ROCK BAND™

GUITAR METHOD

Learn How to Play Electric or Acoustic Guitar
Using Songs from the Popular Video Game!

BY DOUG BODUCH

© 2008 Harmonix Music Systems, Inc. All Rights Reserved.
Harmonix, Rock Band and all related titles and logos are trademarks of Harmonix Music Systems, Inc., an MTV Networks company.
Rock Band developed by Harmonix Music Systems, Inc. MTV: Music Television,
MTV Games and all related titles and logos are trademarks of MTV Networks,
a division of Viacom International Inc.

ISBN 978-1-4234-6230-9

HAL•LEONARD®
CORPORATION

7777 W. BLUEMOUND RD. P.O. BOX 13819 MILWAUKEE, WI 53213

Visit Hal Leonard Online at
www.halleonard.com

INTRODUCTION

Congratulations on your decision to play guitar! It is, by far, the coolest of all the instruments. This book will get you started with the basics and have you playing your favorite songs in no time. You won't even have to learn to read music. The *Rock Band Guitar Method* features a revolutionary tab-only notation system that's guaranteed to speed you on your way to rock stardom. With a great selection of your favorite tunes from the *Rock Band* video game, you'll master all of the techniques of the guitar gods.

The book also includes a CD with audio of all the examples. Use it as a reference to learn the guitar parts and then try your hand at jamming along.

This isn't a "play guitar in five minutes a day" type of approach; those never work. You'll need to put in your practice time to reap the rewards, so be patient. Some techniques might feel very awkward at first. Repetition is the key. Just like playing the video game, you'll want to play these songs over and over.

CONTENTS

CHAPTER 1
GETTING STARTED

Parts of the Guitar

Before you begin playing, it's a good idea to learn the names of the parts of your guitar (as there will be references made to them throughout the book). Even though your guitar may look different than the ones pictured below, its parts should essentially be the same.

Acoustic Guitar

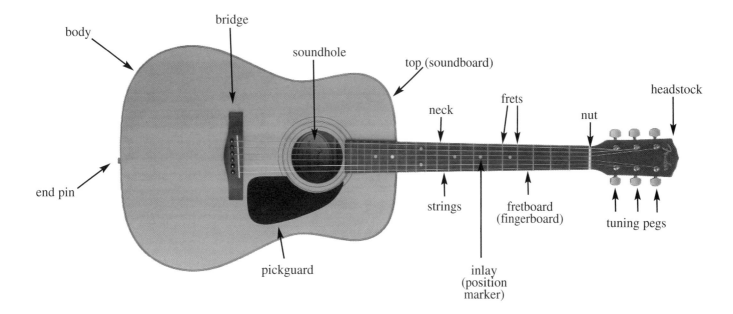

Electric Guitar

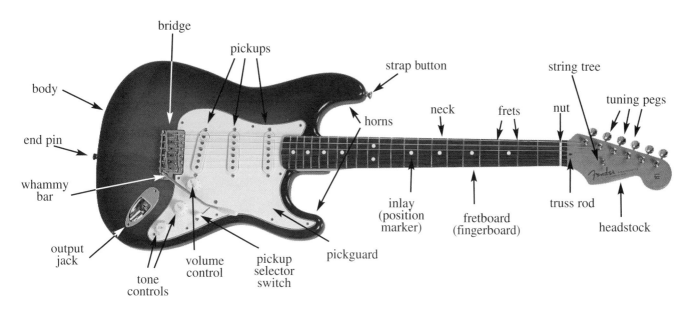

Pitch

The guitar's strings are ordered from the thickest (lowest-sounding string) to the thinnest (highest-sounding string). The difference between these sounds is referred to as *pitch*. When played open (not pressed down at a fret), these pitches are E-A-D-G-B-E, from lowest to highest. Different pitches on each string are produced by depressing the string at a fret. As you move up in frets (from the nut to the bridge), the pitch will get higher.

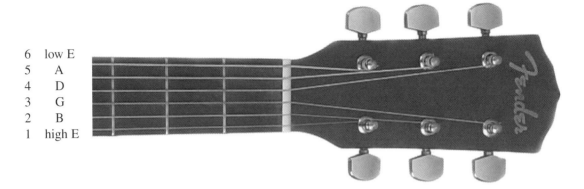

6	low E
5	A
4	D
3	G
2	B
1	high E

Position

Use the pictures below to help find a comfortable playing position. Whether you decide to sit or stand, it's important to remain relaxed and tension-free.

Left-Hand Placement

It's very important to pay close attention to correct left-hand placement. You don't want to develop any bad habits that will be hard to break later. Use the photos below as a guide.

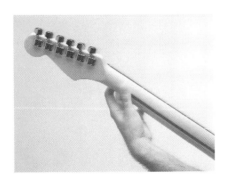

- Make sure your thumb is behind the neck
- Arch your fingers and touch the strings with your fingertips only
- If your finger is too close or too far away from the fret, you'll get a dull or buzzing sound
- Use just enough pressure when fretting a note to achieve a clear, ringing tone

Right-Hand Placement

Hold your pick between your thumb and index finger while keeping the rest of your hand and fingers relaxed. Feel free to rest your hand and fingers on the guitar for support.

Start by simply playing one string with a downward motion of the pick. Next, strum a few strings at once with that same downward motion. This may feel awkward at first, but in time you'll gain more right-hand control. You can also try picking or strumming the strings with an upward motion. Throughout the book, downstrokes will be notated with a ⊓ and upstrokes will be indicated with a V.

Track 1

Tuning

You'll tune your guitar by adjusting the tension of the strings at the tuning pegs. The accompanying CD includes tuning notes, starting with the lowest in pitch (thickest string), E, followed by the A, D, G, B strings, and finally the highest in pitch (thinnest string), E. Pluck each string and compare them to the corresponding pitches on the CD and adjust your tuning pegs accordingly. If your string sounds lower in pitch than the CD, you need to tighten the peg, or turn it counterclockwise. If your string sounds higher in pitch, then you'll need to loosen it by turning the peg clockwise. Always tune the string up, by going lower in pitch and then tightening the peg up to the correct pitch. This helps to take out any slack from the string. Listen for the *beat waves*, a series of pulsating sounds. As you get closer to the correct pitch, the beat waves will get slower. When they stop completely, you're in tune.

Developing your ear to hear these waves may be difficult at first. You may find it easier to tune with an *electronic tuner*. These devices have a meter or lights that indicate when you are at the correct pitch.

Yet another way to tune is called *relative tuning*. In this method, you assume the 6th string (lowest in pitch) is in tune or tune it to a piano, pitch pipe, or some other pitch reference. Then, follow these directions:

- Press the 6th string at the 5th fret. This is A. Tune the open 5th string to this pitch.
- Press the 5th string at the 5th fret. This is D. Tune the open 4th string to this pitch.
- Press the 4th string at the 5th fret. This is G. Tune the open 3rd string to this pitch.
- Press the 3rd string at the 4th fret. This is B. Tune the open 2nd string to this pitch.
- Press the 2nd string at the 5th fret. This is E. Tune the open 1st string to this pitch.

A Note on Practicing

Like getting to the expert level on the *Rock Band* game, playing guitar will take some effort. And much like the game, repetition is key. Play the exercises and songs in the book slowly at first and repeat them until you have them memorized. Keep trying to play them faster, but never sacrifice playing them cleanly for speed. The speed will come in time, so be patient. Also, it's much more beneficial to practice a little bit each day than to not pick up your guitar all week and try to cram your practicing into a four-hour session. Keep your guitar in a place where it's easy to pick up and play as often as you can. Have fun and enjoy the journey!

CHAPTER 2
UNDERSTANDING TABLATURE

Tablature, or "tab," is a guitar-specific notation system used universally in guitar magazines, books, and guitar-related websites. The six horizontal lines represent the six strings of the guitar, with the lowest line being the 6th string (lowest in pitch). Numbers are placed on each line, or string, to indicate which fret to play.

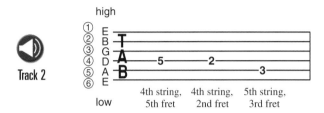

4th string, 4th string, 5th string,
5th fret   2nd fret   3rd fret

If a note is to be played open, or not fretted, a zero (0) will be placed on the line.

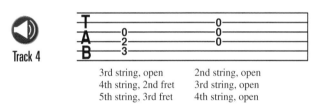

5th string,   1st string,
open   open

If two or more notes are to be played together, or strummed, the numbers will be stacked in a vertical line.

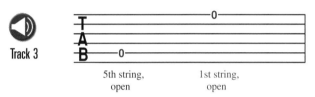

3rd string, open   2nd string, open
4th string, 2nd fret   3rd string, open
5th string, 3rd fret   4th string, open

Another helpful thing to know is that the fingers of your left hand (fretting hand) are numbered one through four when mentioned in the book, as seen here.

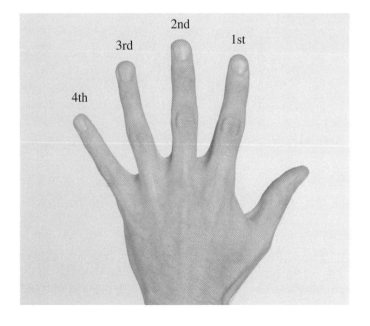

CHAPTER 3
SINGLE NOTES

Playing single notes involves picking one note at a time on a single string.

Start this first example out with your third finger on the 10th fret and use your first finger for the 8th fret. Be sure to listen to the audio example on the CD to get a feel for the rhythm of the notes.

Track 5

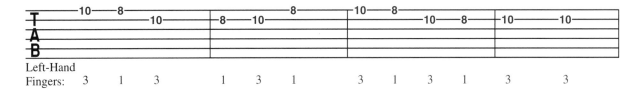

Left-Hand
Fingers: 3   1   3   1   3   1   3   1   3   1   3   3

On this next example, use your second finger for the 2nd fret and third finger for the 3rd fret.

Track 6

Left-Hand
Fingers: 2   2   3   3   2   2   2   3   2

Make sure you're just using your fingertips (not playing "flat-fingered") and you've got your thumb behind the neck for support.

Track 7

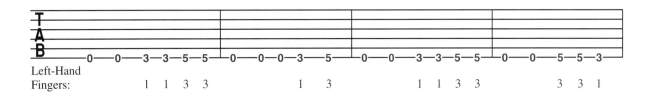

Left-Hand
Fingers: 1   1   3   3   1   3   1   1   3   3   3   3   1

> There are no rules for which fingers to use for each fret. Try to keep your hand in a position that allows you to cover several frets with multiple fingers. Avoid using only one finger and moving your hand around the neck.

Here's an exercise to get all your fingers used to playing single notes. Start with your first finger and then, while keeping your hand in position, use the second, third, and fourth fingers for the following frets. You can lift up each finger after you use it.

Track 8

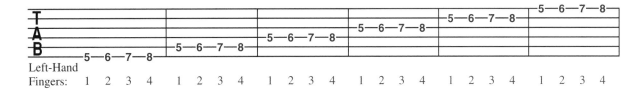

Left-Hand
Fingers: 1 2 3 4   1 2 3 4   1 2 3 4   1 2 3 4   1 2 3 4   1 2 3 4

Many popular songs have signature parts that use single notes. These recognizable sections are referred to as *riffs* or *licks*. The next examples are excerpts from songs that use single notes.

Each song example in the book will have two CD tracks. The first one is a full demonstration with guitar and band. The second track is a "play-along" mix where the main guitar part is taken out so you'll hear only the rhythm section. This will give you a chance to jam along with the band! Practice along with the demo track first before you attempt the second track.

MAPS

Words and Music by Karen Orzolek, Nick Zinner and Brian Chase

Track 9
Demo

Track 10
Play Along

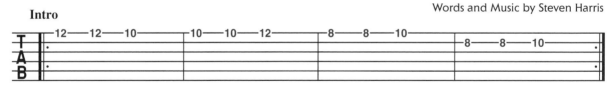

Here is the classic opening riff from Iron Maiden's "Run to the Hills." On the CD, the guitar begins after a short drum intro. It's arranged in a simpler form here, but later in the book you'll learn a technique called *bending* and you'll play it just like the boys from Iron Maiden!

Notice the *repeat signs* ‖::‖. These symbols indicate that you should repeat whatever is in between them.

RUN TO THE HILLS

Words and Music by Steven Harris

Track 11
Demo

Track 12
Play Along

WHEN YOU WERE YOUNG

Words and Music by Brandon Flowers,
Dave Keuning, Mark Stoermer and Ronnie Vannucci

Track 13
Demo

Track 14
Play Along

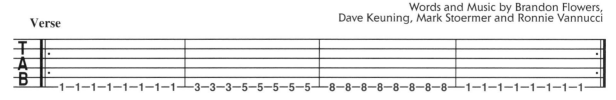

CHAPTER 4
POWER CHORDS

Power chords get their name for two reasons: they sound "powerful" and they give guitar players the "power" to play almost any song. They are, by far, the easiest chords to play, consisting of only two notes—the root (which names the chord) and the fifth scale degree. For this reason, you'll often see these chords referred to as "5" chords written like this: C5, E5, G5, etc. Start by learning three power chords in the open position. You'll need to strum through both strings, sounding the notes together. Make sure you only strike these two strings with the pick.

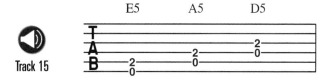

Chord Diagrams

In addition to tablature, sometimes a *chord diagram* will be used to show finger placement for chords. A *chord diagram* is like standing your guitar up and looking straight at the neck. The 6th string (lowest in pitch) will be the line on the left, with the 1st string (highest in pitch) over to the right. The frets are the horizontal lines, with the heavy line on top representing the nut. The black dots indicate where to place your fingers. If a string is to be played open, an "O" symbol is shown above it. If the string is not to be played, an "X" is shown above it. The numbers below the diagram indicate which left-hand fingers to use.

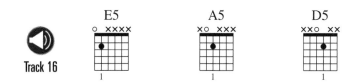

Now try these chords in a few exercises.

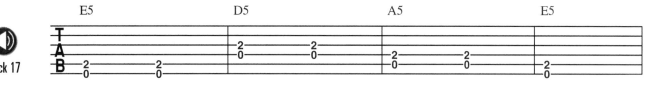

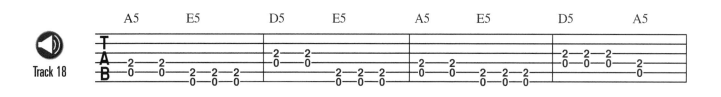

You can also play power chords using two fretted notes. These are a bit trickier than the open-position chords, since you'll be using two left-hand fingers. Use your first finger for the lower note, and either your third or fourth finger (depending on how well you can stretch) for the higher note. The abbreviation "fr" in the chord diagrams is used to indicate higher positions on the neck, and stands for "fret."

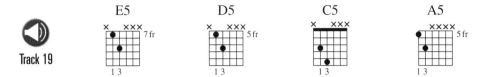

Eventually you'll want to get comfortable playing these with your third finger, but it will take some time for the hand to develop a good stretch. In fact, seasoned players can actually reach these chords with their first and second fingers! Again, the lower note names the chord, so try and get familiar with each chord's name as you play them.

Another cool thing about these chords is that they are movable, so you can move them up and down the neck and create all kinds of riffs! Here are some exercises to get you started.

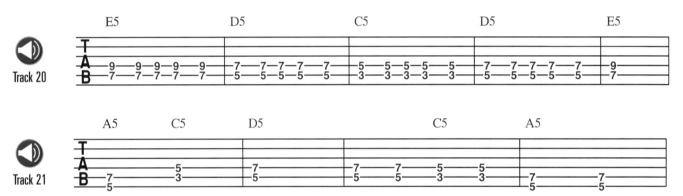

It's time to use these power chords in a song. When switching from chord to chord, try and keep your fingers in the same "power-chord position." If two chords are on the same strings, just lift up your fingers slightly and slide them to the next position. Remember to listen to the accompanying CD to hear the rhythms.

IN BLOOM

Words and Music by Kurt Cobain

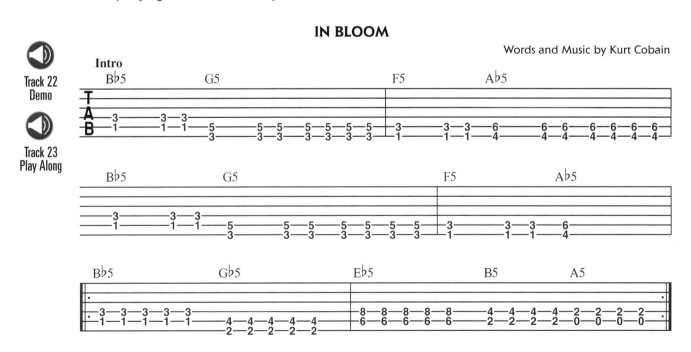

Power chords can also be played with three notes. These chords add a note an *octave*, or eight scale degrees, above the root note. You can either play these chords with separate fingers, or you can *barre* the notes by laying one finger flat across the strings to hold down both notes. Here are some of the power chords you learned earlier, now played with three notes.

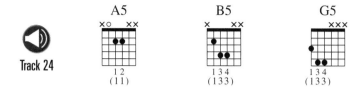

Now try some exercises featuring a variety of three-note power chords.

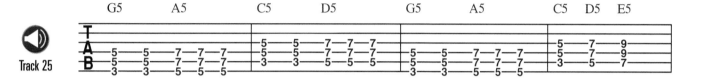

The vertical lines in the tablature separate the music into *measures*. If a note or notes are to be held or sustained for more than one measure, they will be in parentheses. Do not pick or strum the notes in parentheses, simply let them continue ringing.

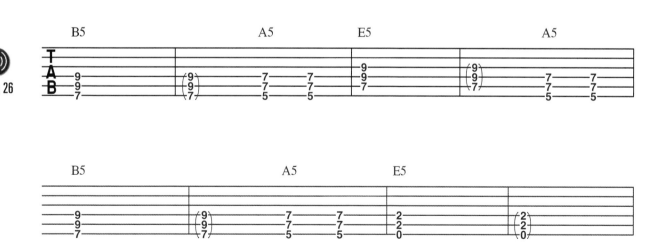

Here's a classic from KISS that features a great single-note riff intro as well as some power chords.

DETROIT ROCK CITY

Words and Music by Paul Stanley and Bob Ezrin

Track 27
Demo

Track 28
Play Along

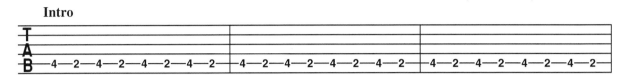

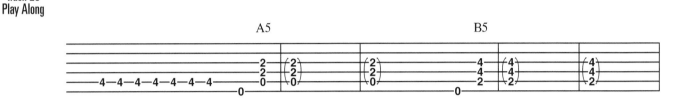

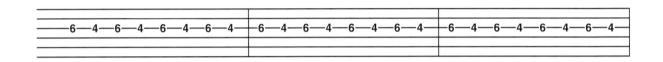

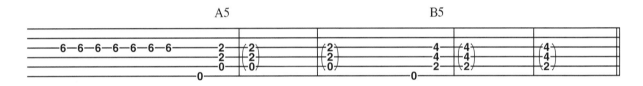

As you can see, three-note power chords just add one note to the two-note chords you learned before. They are a bit more difficult to finger, but they do have a fuller sound. Go back and try using the three-note power chords in place of the two-note chords in the previous exercises.

CHAPTER 5
OPEN-POSITION CHORDS

Open-position chords can be found in every style of music, and are played not only on acoustic guitar, but also electric. In general, these are the chords you'll use when you strum the guitar. Let's start with some basic major chords.

Track 29

Make sure you're only using your fingertips to fret these chords. If you play "flat-fingered," you may block other strings from sounding. Play through each note of the chord individually to ensure that all notes are sounding clearly. You may need to adjust your hand position.

> The F chord uses a technique called the *barre*, discussed briefly in the previous chapter. In the F chord, your first finger will fret both the first and second strings at the first fret. This is a tough technique to get, and it may take some time to become proficient. If you find it too difficult right now, simply don't play the first string.

Now try these chords in a few exercises. Changing from chord to chord will be difficult, at first. You'll have long gaps of time in between chords. Eventually, these gaps will get shorter and soon you'll be changing chords right in time with the music. To help eliminate the gaps, memorize each chord fingering and try to visualize where your fingers need to be before changing to the next chord. Remember the chord by its name so you don't have to rely on the tab. Use downstrokes throughout to strum the chords.

Track 30

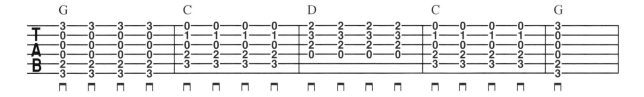

Track 31

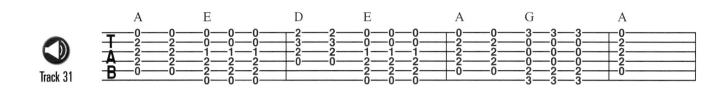

Track 32

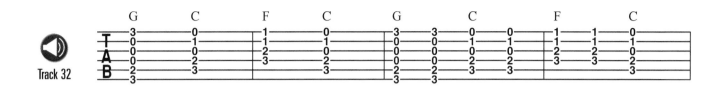

Another type of chord is the *minor chord*. These chords will be notated with an "m" next to the chord name (Am, Em, etc.) and will have a darker, more sad quality. Here are some common open-position minor chords.

Track 33

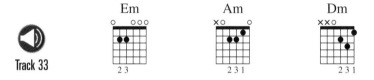

Here are some exercises using both major and minor chords.

Track 34

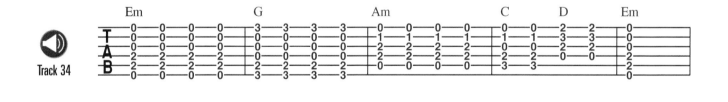

Track 35

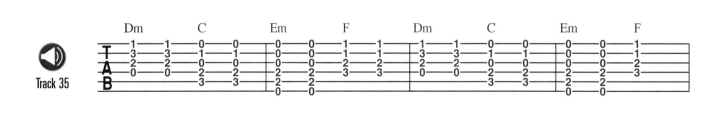

"Should I Stay or Should I Go" uses four major chords—D, G, A, and F.

SHOULD I STAY OR SHOULD I GO

Words and Music by Mick Jones and Joe Strummer

Track 36
Demo

Track 37
Play Along

In the next song, we use some open-position chords along with a quick riff at the end.

WANTED DEAD OR ALIVE

Words and Music by Jon Bon Jovi and Richie Sambora

Track 38
Demo

Track 39
Play Along

Strum Patterns

In the previous examples, you only used downstrokes to strum the chords. *Strum patterns* are simply rhythmic variations that our right hand will follow, catching the strings on both down and upstrokes. A downstroke will be notated with a ⊓ and an upstroke will be notated with a ∨.

Track 40

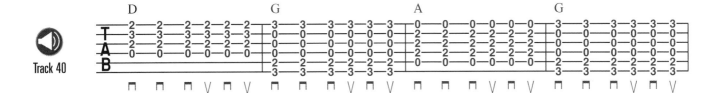

Although this is a popular strum pattern, it is not the only one. The rhythmic variations are end-less. Using the chords you learned, try and come up with some of your own strum patterns.

CHAPTER 6
ARPEGGIOS

An *arpeggio* is simply defined as the notes of a chord played individually. Take the C chord we learned in Chapter 5 and try playing it as an arpeggio.

Track 41

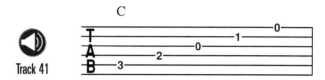

Playing arpeggios is a great way to see if all the notes of the chord are ringing clearly. Try the next example.

Track 42

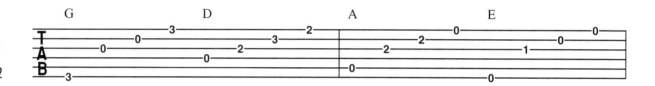

> When you play arpeggios, try to let all the notes ring together. Make sure that your fingers don't accidentally mute a string and stop it from ringing.

Arpeggios can also be different patterns of notes, rather than just ascending from lowest to highest.

Track 43

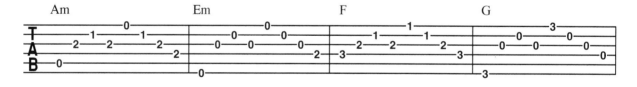

When you encounter two or more strings that descend, you may find it easier to play those notes with a series of upstrokes.

Track 44

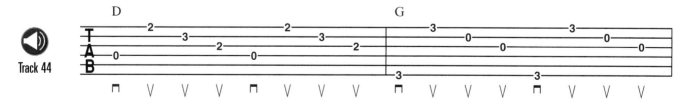

Now try these arpeggio ideas in some popular songs. Remember to listen to the CD to get a feel for the rhythms.

WANTED DEAD OR ALIVE

Words and Music by Jon Bon Jovi and Richie Sambora

Track 45
Demo

Track 46
Play Along

Intro

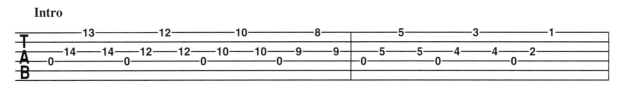

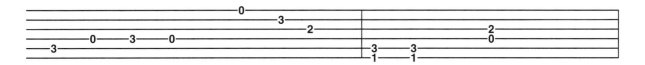

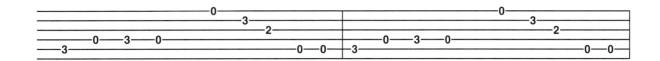

DON'T FEAR THE REAPER

Words and Music by Donald Roeser

Track 47
Demo

Track 48
Play Along

Intro

play 8 times

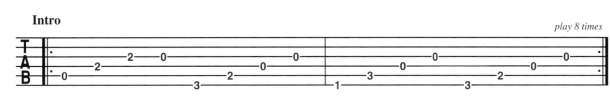

CHAPTER 7
PALM AND FRET-HAND MUTING

Sometimes in a song you'll hear what sounds like a click or "chucka" sound. This is referred to as *fret-hand muting* and is a very simple technique. Lay the fingers of your fret hand over the strings, touching them lightly, but not depressing them enough to touch the frets. Then strum through the strings with your pick hand as you normally would. The sound produced should be similar to that of a snare drum. You should not be able to hear any pitch.

Track 49

In tablature, fret-hand muting will be notated with an "X" on the strings used.

The song "Creep" uses some very obvious fret-hand muting right before the chorus.

CREEP

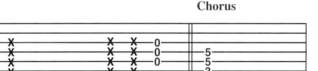

Track 50
Demo

Track 51
Play Along

Another type of muting is called *palm muting*. This is that chunky sound you often hear with power chords. Palm muting involves laying the pad, or fleshy part of your pick hand, over the strings where they meet the bridge. Keep your hand in contact with the strings and pick normally.

Track 52

Palm muting is notated with a "P.M." underneath the tab and a dotted line indicating how long the palm muting is to be executed.

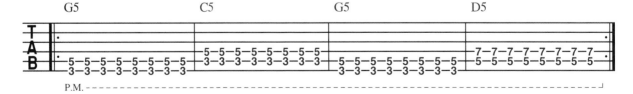

Track 53

> If your hand is moved back too far, you won't get any palm muting. If it's too far up, or closer to the neck, you'll get too much and won't be able to distinguish any pitch. Play around with your position to achieve the perfect blend.

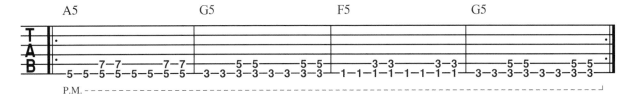

Here are some rock classics that use palm muting.

PARANOID

Words and Music by Anthony Iommi,
John Osbourne, William Ward and Terence Butler

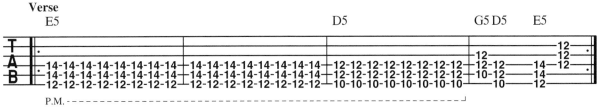

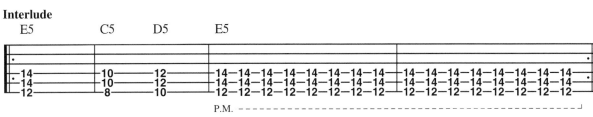

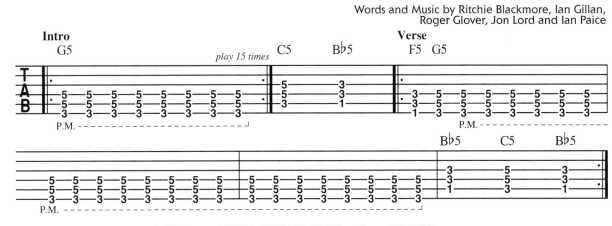

Many times a palm-muted part will be followed by a section that doesn't have palm muting.
This is a great way to add punch and energy. Simply lift your palm up and strum normally for
those non–palm muted parts and they should jump to life!

HIGHWAY STAR

Words and Music by Ritchie Blackmore, Ian Gillan,
Roger Glover, Jon Lord and Ian Paice

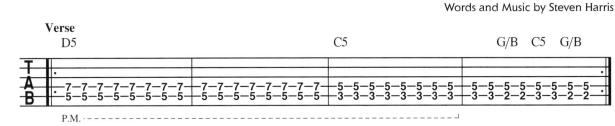

RUN TO THE HILLS

Words and Music by Steven Harris

CHAPTER 8
BARRE CHORDS

Back in Chapter 5, you learned the F chord which uses a barre across two strings. This next group of chords you'll learn uses a full barre across all six strings. The technique is tough, but the rewards are big. Barring across all six strings means these chords are movable up the neck. So by learning one chord, you really know twelve!

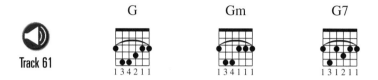

Make sure you keep your first finger as straight as possible when you barre. It might help to roll it a bit to the thumb side and play more on the bony part of the finger.

The root note on the 6th string names the chord. So if you need a G♯ chord, simply move the G chord up one fret.

Here are a few exercises using these six-string barre chords.

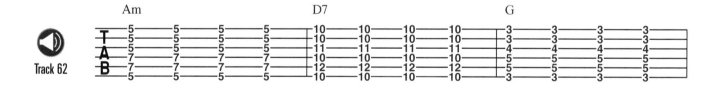

This one has some fret-hand muting.

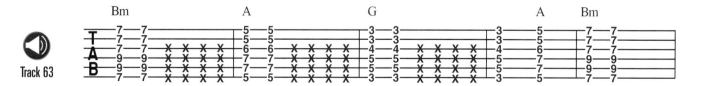

Barre chords can also be played with roots on the 5th string. The fingerings are different, but the technique and theory are the same.

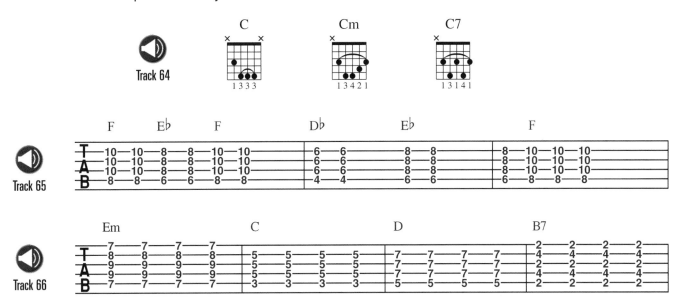

By learning these six chord fingerings (5th- and 6th-string roots) and having the ability to move the chords around on the neck, you now know 72 new chords! Here are a few popular songs to try them in.

ARE YOU GONNA BE MY GIRL

Words and Music by Nic Cester and Cameron Muncey

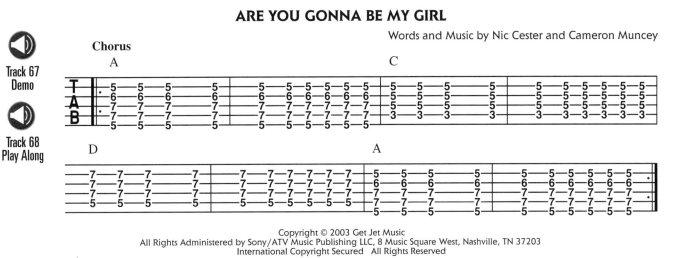

"Long Time" has a section that uses barre chords with some of the fret-hand muting you learned in Chapter 7.

LONG TIME

Words and Music by Tom Scholz

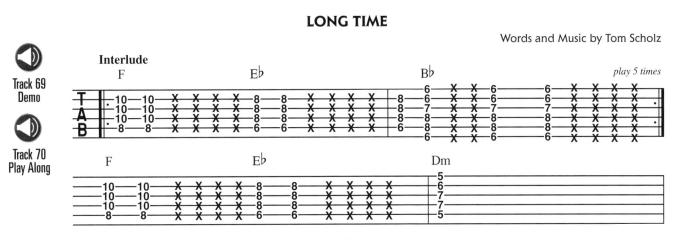

"Creep" uses some barre chords played as arpeggios. Again, this is a great way to see if all the notes are ringing clearly.

CREEP

Words and Music by Albert Hammond,
Mike Hazlewood, Thomas Yorke, Richard Greenwood,
Philip Selway, Colin Greenwood and Edward O'Brian

Verse

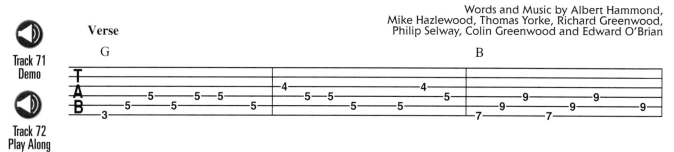

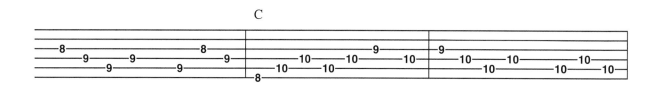

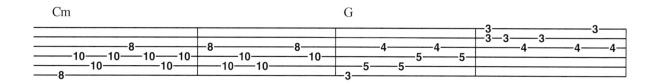

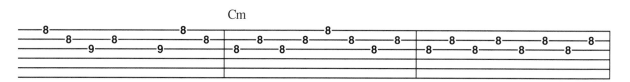

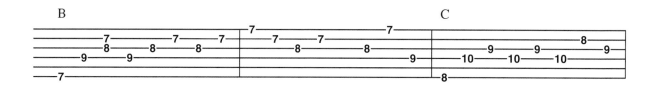

It's important to know these chords by their name instead of just the tab numbers, so you'll need to become familiar with the notes on the 5th and 6th strings. Below is a chart which will serve as a good reference.

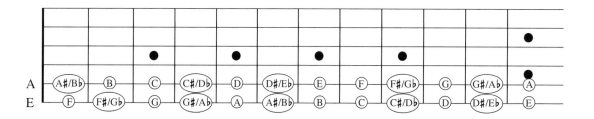

CHAPTER 9
HAMMER-ONS, PULL-OFFS, AND SLIDES

A *hammer-on* involves picking one note and then coming down with a left-hand finger to sound a higher note, on the same string, without picking. In the tab, it will be notated with a curved line connecting both notes (known as a *slur*). Again, only pick the first note and hammer on with a different left-hand finger to sound the second note.

Track 73

A *pull-off* is basically the reverse of a hammer-on and involves two notes that descend on the same string. Pick the first one, pull down with the fretting finger, and then lift off to sound the second note without picking. You'll need to have both fingers on the string in order to do a pull-off. Again, it will be notated by a curved line in the tab.

Track 74

Here are some exercises that mix up both hammer-ons and pull-offs. Remember, a hammer-on will always ascend, while a pull-off will descend.

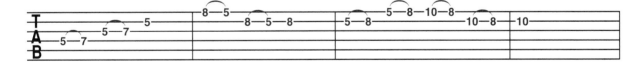

Track 75

Track 76

The intro to "Paranoid" is a great example of hammer-ons. In the first measure, play a small barre chord with your first finger at the 12th fret and hammer on to the 14th fret with your third finger. The hammer-on creates an E5 power chord.

PARANOID

Words and Music by Anthony Iommi, John Osbourne, William Ward and Terence Butler

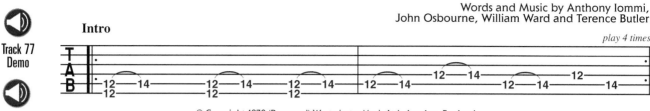

Slides are another way of connecting two notes on the same string. Simply pick the first note and—while keeping pressure on the string—slide your finger up or down to the next note. Slides will be notated with a slanted line. An additional curved line (slur) indicates that only the first note is picked.

Here are a few exercises to get you familiar with slides.

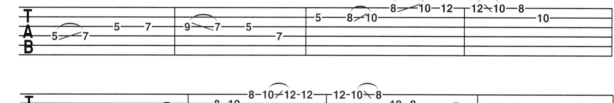

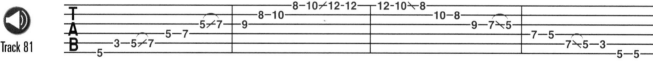

The interlude section to "Detroit Rock City" makes good use of slides.

DETROIT ROCK CITY

Words and Music by Paul Stanley and Bob Ezrin

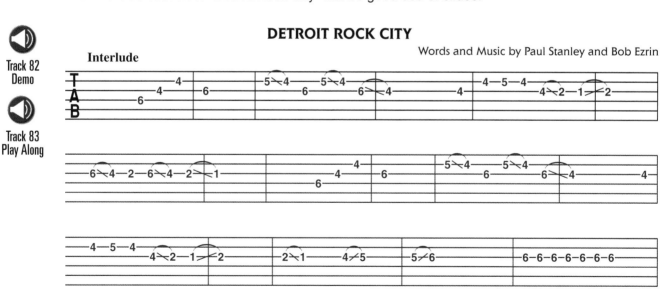

Track 77
Demo

Track 78
Play Along

Track 79

Track 80

Track 81

Track 82
Demo

Track 83
Play Along

Getting Faster

It's important to develop speed on the guitar. You'll get it naturally over time, but there are a few things you can do to help the process along.

- Practice slowly and precisely at first, never play sloppy
- Memorize the part
- Use *alternate picking* (down and upstrokes in combination)
- Use a *metronome* (essential time-keeping tool for all musicians)

This excerpt from the solo in "Highway Star" is a great exercise in speed development.

HIGHWAY STAR

Words and Music by Ritchie Blackmore, Ian Gillan,
Roger Glover, Jon Lord and Ian Paice

Track 84
Demo

Track 85
Play Along

Guitar Solo

```
5—6—8—8—5—6—8—8—5—6—8—8—5—6—8—8 | 5—6—8—8—5—6—8—8—5—6—8—8—5—6—8—8
```

```
6—8—10-10—6—8—10-10—6—8—10-10—6—8—10-10 | 6—8—10-10—6—8—10-10—6—8—10-10—6—8—10-10
```

```
8—10-12-12—8—10-12-12—8—10-12-12—8—10-12-12 | 8—10-12-12—8—10-12-12—8—10-12-12—8—10-12-12
```

```
17-17—0—0—15-15—0—0—14-14—0—0—12-12—0—0 | 11-11—0—0—10-10—0—0—9—9—0—0—8—8—0—0
```

CHAPTER 10
BENDING

Bending involves raising the pitch of a note by pushing, or stretching, the string up toward the ceiling or down toward the floor. Start off using your third finger and have your first and second finger behind it for support. A bend will be notated in the tab with an arrow.

Track 86

It's important to be aware of pitch when you bend. The number next to the arrowhead indicates how far to bend. For example, a half-step bend equals the distance of one fret. In the next example, pick the first note and then bend the second note up to the same pitch.

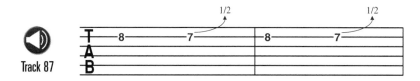

Track 87

A one-step bend equals the distance of two frets. Before bending the note in the next example, pick the note two frets up and use that as your target note for pitch.

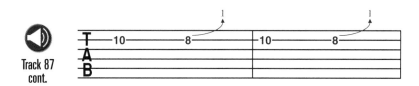

Track 87
cont.

Here are some exercises to get you used to bending.

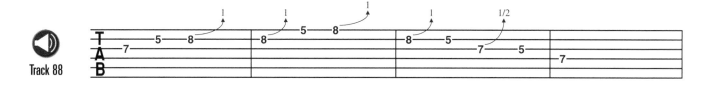

Track 88

An arrow pointing downward means that the bend is released and brought back to the starting note.

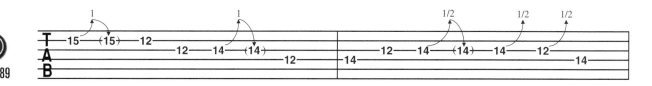

Track 89

26

The intro to "Run to the Hills" uses *unison bends* (one note is held static while the other note is bent). Once bent, both notes should have the same pitch. Your first finger will be playing a different string, but you can still use your second finger for support on the bend. On the CD, the guitar begins after a short drum intro.

RUN TO THE HILLS

Words and Music by Steven Harris

 Track 90 Demo

 Track 91 Play Along

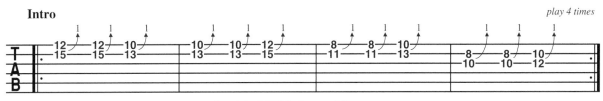

The solo for "Highway Star" is another good study in bending. Remember to pay attention to the pitch of the notes you bend.

HIGHWAY STAR

Words and Music by Ritchie Blackmore, Ian Gillan,
Roger Glover, Jon Lord and Ian Paice

 Track 92 Demo

 Track 93 Play Along

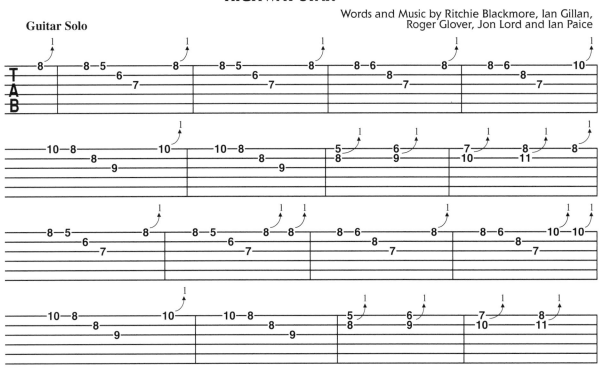

The intro solo to "Long Time" uses bends as well as the hammer-ons, pull-offs, and slides learned in the previous chapter.

LONG TIME

Words and Music by Tom Scholz

 Track 94 Demo

 Track 95 Play Along

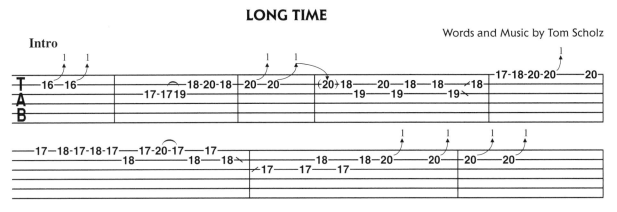

CHAPTER 11
PUTTING IT ALL TOGETHER

You've learned quite a few techniques over the course of this *Rock Band Method.* Following are two full songs that employ many of the topics you've studied. Remember that repetitive practice is the key. Play slowly at first until you have the parts ingrained in your fingers.

SAY IT AIN'T SO

Performance Notes

- Make sure the arpeggio rings clear in the intro.
- Listen to the audio to hear how the verse part rests in between the chords. You'll need to stop the notes from ringing by using either your fret or pick hand.
- Kick on *distortion* for the chorus, bridge, and guitar solo. Distortion is the dirty guitar tone associated with rock and metal.
- The guitar solo has some bends, hammer-ons, and pull-offs. Make sure the bends are in tune and practice any fast parts slowly at first.

Track 96
Demo

Track 97
Play Along

Intro

Words and Music by Rivers Cuomo

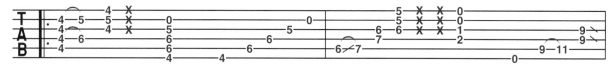

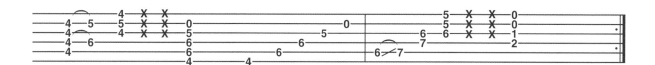

Verse   **Chorus**

play 8 times

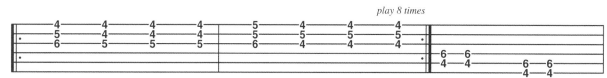

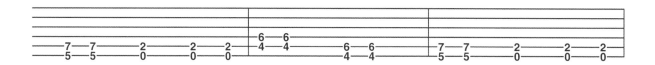

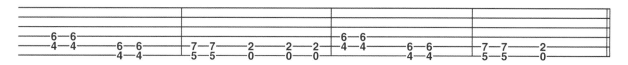

Interlude

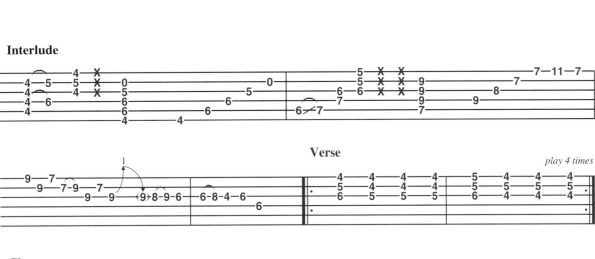

Verse

play 4 times

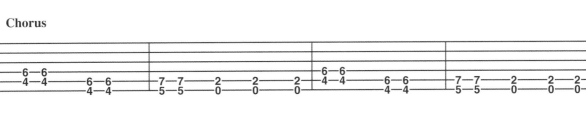

Chorus

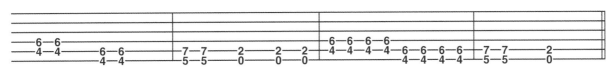

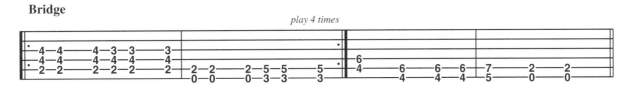

Bridge

play 4 times

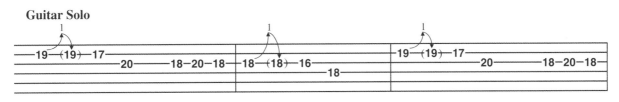

Guitar Solo

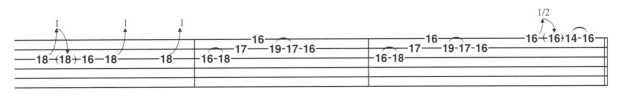

Chorus

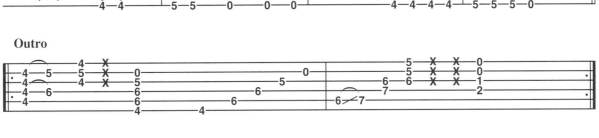

Outro

MISSISSIPPI QUEEN

Performance Notes

- Use distortion throughout the song.
- Make sure all those bends are in tune.
- If a tab number has an arrow pointing straight up, that indicates a *pre-bend*, which means you pick the note while it is still bent.
- Keep pressure on the strings when you slide.
- On the CD, the guitar begins after a short cowbell intro.

Words and Music by Leslie West,
Felix Pappalardi, Corky Laing and David Rea

**Track 98
Demo**

**Track 99
Play Along**

Intro

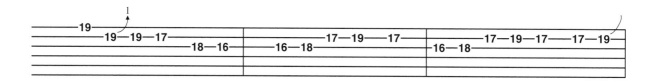

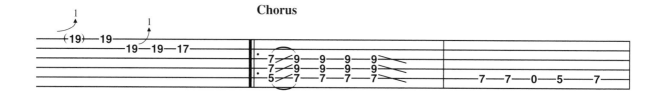

Chorus

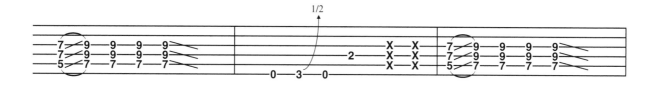

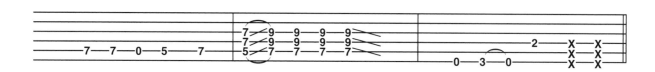

Verse

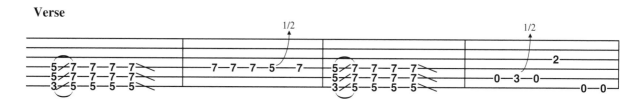

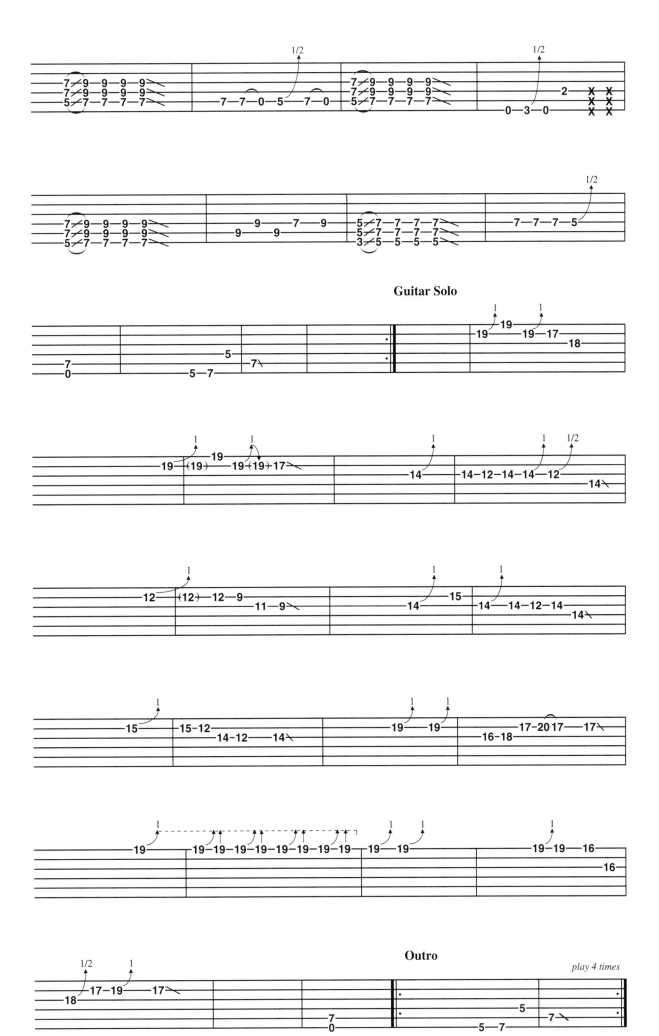

Guitar Solo

Outro

play 4 times

Hal Leonard is proud to present these outstanding songbooks featuring the hits from the wildly popular video game phenomenom. Choose a book and rock the guitar, bass, drums, or vocals on your favorite songs!

GUITAR METHOD
by Doug Boduch

This method is designed for anyone just learning to play acoustic or electric guitar. It is based on years of teaching guitar students of all ages, and it's the perfect guide to help make the transition from the video game console to a guitar fun and easy. Songs include: Creep • Don't Fear the Reaper • Mississippi Queen • Say It Ain't So • Wanted Dead or Alive • When You Were Young • and more!

00696053 Book/CD Pack.....................................$12.95
00696054 Book Only...$5.95

PIANO/VOCAL/GUITAR

25 piano/vocal/guitar arrangements, including: Are You Gonna Be My Girl • Black Hole Sun • Dani California • Detroit Rock City • Don't Fear the Reaper • Mississippi Queen • Paranoid • Should I Stay or Should I Go • Suffragette City • Wanted Dead or Alive • Welcome Home • Won't Get Fooled Again • and more!

00311736 .... $19.95

EASY GUITAR WITH NOTES AND TAB

Includes 25 songs: Are You Gonna Be My Girl • Creep • Don't Fear the Reaper • Learn to Fly • Long Time • Maps • Paranoid • Should I Stay or Should I Go • Suffragette City • Wanted Dead or Alive • Welcome Home • When You Were Young • and more!

00702242 .... $19.95

GUITAR PLAY-ALONG VOLUME 97

The Guitar Play-Along series will help you play your favorite songs quickly and easily! Just follow the tab, listen to the CD to hear how the guitar should sound, and then play along using the separate backing tracks. 8 songs: Are You Gonna Be My Girl • Black Hole Sun • Creep • Dani California • In Bloom • Learn to Fly • Say It Ain't So • When You Were Young.

00700703 Book/CD Pack $14.95

GUITAR RECORDED VERSIONS

25 transcriptions in notes and tab, including: Are You Gonna Be My Girl • Black Hole Sun • Dani California • Detroit Rock City • Don't Fear the Reaper • Mississippi Queen • Paranoid • Should I Stay or Should I Go • Suffragette City • Wanted Dead or Alive • Welcome Home • Won't Get Fooled Again • and more.

00690934...$24.95

ROCK BAND 2 GUITAR RECORDED VERSIONS

39 more songs from the hit game, including: American Woman • Aqualung • Carry on Wayward Son • Come Out and Play • Eye of the Tiger • Livin' on a Prayer • Pinball Wizard • Ramblin' Man • Spirit in the Sky • We Got the Beat • White Wedding • You Oughta Know • and more.

00690965..$29.95

BASS PLAY-ALONG VOLUME 21

The Bass Play-Along series will help you play your favorite songs quickly and easily! Just follow the tab, listen to the CD to hear how the bass should sound, and then play along using the separate backing tracks. 8 songs, including: Are You Gonna Be My Girl • Black Hole Sun • Creep • Dani California • In Bloom • Learn to Fly • Say It Ain't So • When You Were Young.

00700705 Book/CD Pack $14.95

BASS RECORDED VERSIONS

25 bass transcriptions, including: Are You Gonna Be My Girl • Black Hole Sun • Dani California • Detroit Rock City • Don't Fear the Reaper • Mississippi Queen • Paranoid • Should I Stay or Should I Go • Suffragette City • Wanted Dead or Alive • Welcome Home • Won't Get Fooled Again • and more.

00690946..$22.95

DRUM PLAY-ALONG VOLUME 19

The Drum Play-Along series will help you play your favorite songs quickly and easily! Just follow the drum notation, listen to the CD to hear how the drums should sound, and then play along using the separate backing tracks. Includes 8 songs: Are You Gonna Be My Girl • Black Hole Sun • Creep • Dani California • In Bloom • Learn to Fly • Say It Ain't So • When You Were Young.

00700707 Book/CD Pack $14.95

DRUM RECORDED VERSIONS

25 transcriptions: Are You Gonna Be My Girl • Black Hole Sun • Dani California • Detroit Rock City • Don't Fear the Reaper • Mississippi Queen • Paranoid • Should I Stay or Should I Go • Suffragette City • Wanted Dead or Alive • Won't Get Fooled Again • and more.

00690947 .... $22.95

VOCAL

Lead sheets for 25 songs, including: Are You Gonna Be My Girl • Black Hole Sun • Dani California • Detroit Rock City • Don't Fear the Reaper • Mississippi Queen • Paranoid • Should I Stay or Should I Go • Suffragette City • Wanted Dead or Alive • Welcome Home • Won't Get Fooled Again • and more!

00311737 .... $12.95

HAL•LEONARD®
CORPORATION
7777 W. BLUEMOUND RD. P.O. BOX 13819
MILWAUKEE, WISCONSIN 53213

www.halleonard.com

0908